My ANIMAL FAMILY

Kate Peridot

Illustrated by Nic Jones

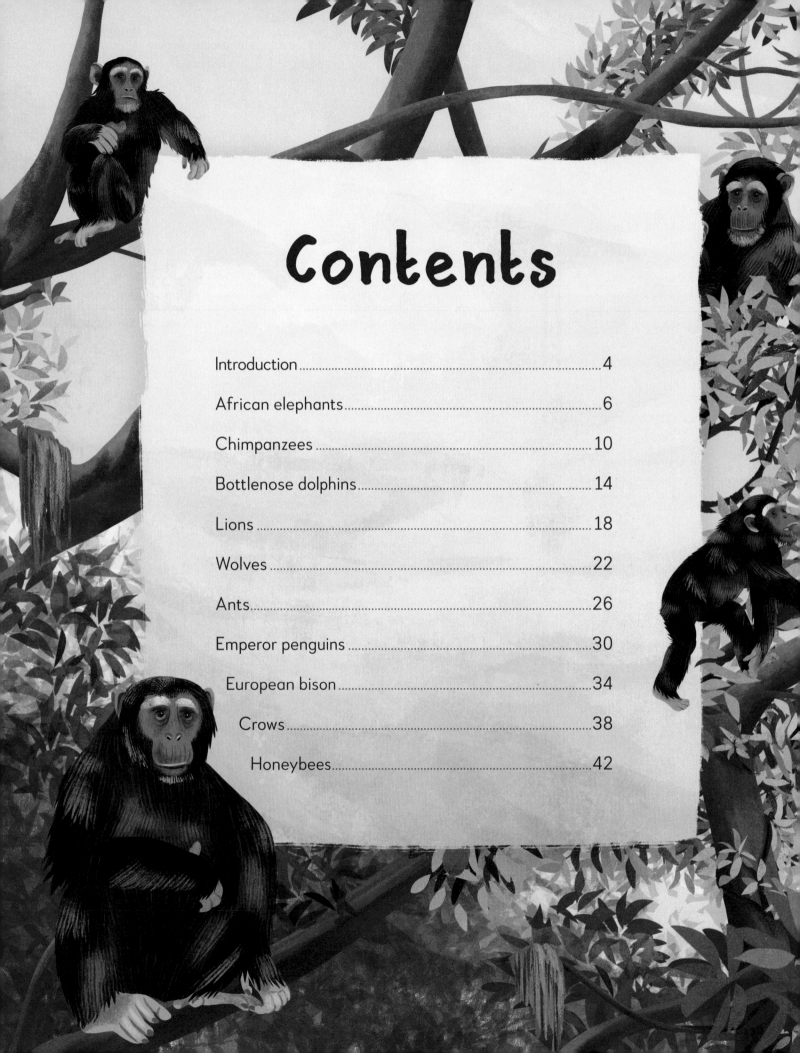

Contents

Introduction

Animals have families and live in groups, just as we do. These families and communities can be very different from one another.

Turn the pages to meet **15 animals** and their **families**, including...

Honeybees

African elephants

Lions

European bison

Wolves

Find out **who's in charge**, whose job it is to find the food, how they care for and **protect** one another, and how they **communicate** using sounds, smells, and body language.

Bottlenose dolphins

Crows

Orangutans

Can you spot any **similarities** and **differences** in your own family?

Seahorses

Emperor penguins

African elephants

We are a matriarchal society.

Matriarch

Other herd

Hyena

Calf

My mom is the leader of our herd. She is the oldest and wisest cow. She remembers where the water holes are and when our favorite fruit ripens. She knows the way across the savanna, and the smell of danger. She keeps us safe and teaches us the way of the elephant.

Our herd is made up of mothers, daughters, sisters, aunts, and calves. If there are lions or hyenas prowling, we make a protective circle around the calves. When our herd grows too big, we split into two herds for a while to find more food. But we always keep in touch. A female elephant never forgets her family.

When my brother was fourteen years old, he left the herd, but he didn't go very far away. Sometimes young bull elephants hang out together, but they aren't loyal to each other. They fight to prove who is the strongest, and only the strongest bulls will find a mate.

Calf

We talk with other elephants in lots of ways: **trumpeting** and **rumbling**, touching and stamping, flicking our tails, and curling our ears. When we feel threatened, we raise our trunks, stick out our ears, and **charge!**

FACT FILE

Name of group: Herd
Size of group: 8-100
Fact: Elephant rumbling sounds travel great distances. The shape and positioning of elephant ears help to catch these low-frequency calls. Elephants also sense the vibrations through their feet.

Young bulls

"We've found a watering hole. Come and join the party!"

Alpha
male

To remind other chimpanzees who's in
charge, the alpha male beats the ground,
raises his arms, and stares at them.

Chimpanzees

We are a patriarchal society.

I am the alpha male—the strongest and smartest chimpanzee in our troop. I am in charge of my territory, and I will fight any chimpanzee who challenges me. I choose other loyal males to maintain order, boss the females around and, protect everyone from predators.

"It's hard work being the alpha male!"

Challenger

If another chimpanzee tries to challenge me, I will beat them with my fists, bite, and chase them. Our **screams** and **howls** carry great distances through the forest, so other troops know we are there.

Our community is large and includes lots of family groups. We don't hang out with each other every day. Families or individuals can wander off to find food as long as they stay in my territory and come when I call.

"We like being in a community, and it makes us feel safe."

The females take care of the infants while I guard the troop with the help of the other males. Male chimps stay in the troop they were born into, but fully grown females often leave to join other troops.

FACT FILE

Name of group: Troop
Size of group: 15-120
Fact: A successful alpha male must control his aggression and rule fairly. Otherwise, other strong males will team up and overthrow him.

Bottlenose dolphins

We are free spirits!

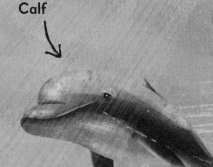

Calf

We live in groups called pods. After I was born I stayed with my mom in a nursery pod for six years. The strongest, most experienced female is in charge, but all the female dolphins work together to take care of the calves. Whenever a dolphin is expecting a baby, she returns to the pod she was born into.

When I was old enough, I started a new pod with my friends. We explored the oceans and learned to hunt. But if we want to swim with our mothers again, we'll always be welcomed back into their pod.

Lead
female

15

Now that I am fully grown, it's just me and my best friend in a male pod. We join other male pods from time to time, to hunt and compete. We love being sociable, and work as a pair to impress the females!

Young male

Every dolphin has a unique sound, and communicates with **whistles** and **clicks**. Us males like to prove who's the boss by biting, chasing, jaw clapping, smacking our tails on the water, emitting bubble clouds, and body slamming. Ouch!

FACT FILE
Name of group: Pod
Size of group: 2-30
Fact: Dolphins are one of the few wild mammals who appear to enjoy spending time with other species, such as whales and humans.

Other pod

Sometimes lots of pods join together for a while and become a super pod.

"Want to play seaweed flick and catch?"

Zebra

Lead
lioness

Lions

We are a team—mostly!

I am the oldest lioness in our pride, and I am in charge of the hunt. Antelope, zebra, and wildebeest are fast and hard to catch, and their kick can be bone-crushing, so it's not easy!

"Through play, we practice our stalking, hunting, and fighting skills."

Cubs

Male

All of the lionesses work together to bring down large prey.

Sometimes the lion hunts too, but he's not as good as us lionesses. He's bigger but slower, and the prey sees him coming! His job is to defend the pride and the pride's territory from other aggressive male lions. He marks the ground with urine, and **ROARS** menacingly to frighten intruders.

After the hunt, the lion eats first, followed by the lionesses who caught the prey. Then the other lionesses eat, and the cubs eat last of all. There's lots of squabbling!

If our pride gets too big and there isn't enough food to hunt, we'll push out the weakest lionesses. I know it's tough, but that's survival. Sometimes lone lionesses will find each other and start a new pride.

My sons left the pride when they were two years old. They will stay in an all-male pride until they are strong enough to challenge a lion in charge of a female pride. If they win the fight, they will take over the protection of the lionesses and have their own cubs.

Departing lioness

A male lion will swat or gently bite others to remind them of their place. When we are relaxed, we greet each other with soft **hums** and **puffs**.

When lions feel threatened, they make themselves look as big as possible by lifting their tail, hunching their backs, and showing their teeth.

Den

Beta

Wolves

We are a structured family.

My parents are the alpha pair in charge of our pack. When I was a young pup, I stayed in the den with my mom, brother, and sister while my dad led the hunt. Once we were old enough, we left the den and wandered with the pack, following the movements of the deer, caribou, and elk. We were still too young to hunt large animals, so we waited at a meeting point guarded by my aunt, the beta wolf, who is second in command.

Alpha pair →

"The alpha pair stays together for life and teaches its family everything it needs to know to hunt and survive."

When the pack returns with food, the young cubs eat first with our parents, then the beta wolf, then my grownup brothers and sisters, and lastly the omega wolf. The omega is the lowest ranking wolf, but also the most playful. We practice our hunting and fighting skills with him, and he doesn't mind losing.

When I am old enough, I will leave my pack and search for a mate by **howling**. Hopefully, another wolf will answer my call, and together we will become the next alpha pair and start our own pack.

A wolf pack has a very close bond. We show our loyalty to one another by rubbing shoulders and giving each other a quick lick. My parents remind the pack they are in charge by standing tall, raising their tail high, pointing their ears, snarling, or laying their head on the top of a wolf's back. The lower ranked wolf cowers, whimpers, tucks in his tail, and rolls on his back to show he is submissive.

A wolf's howl can be heard across great distances

Omega

FACT FILE

Name of group: Pack

Size of group: 2-30

Fact: Wolves have a powerful sense of smell. They have scent glands on the back of their tails and between the toes on their feet. They recognize each other's scent and can track prey over huge distances.

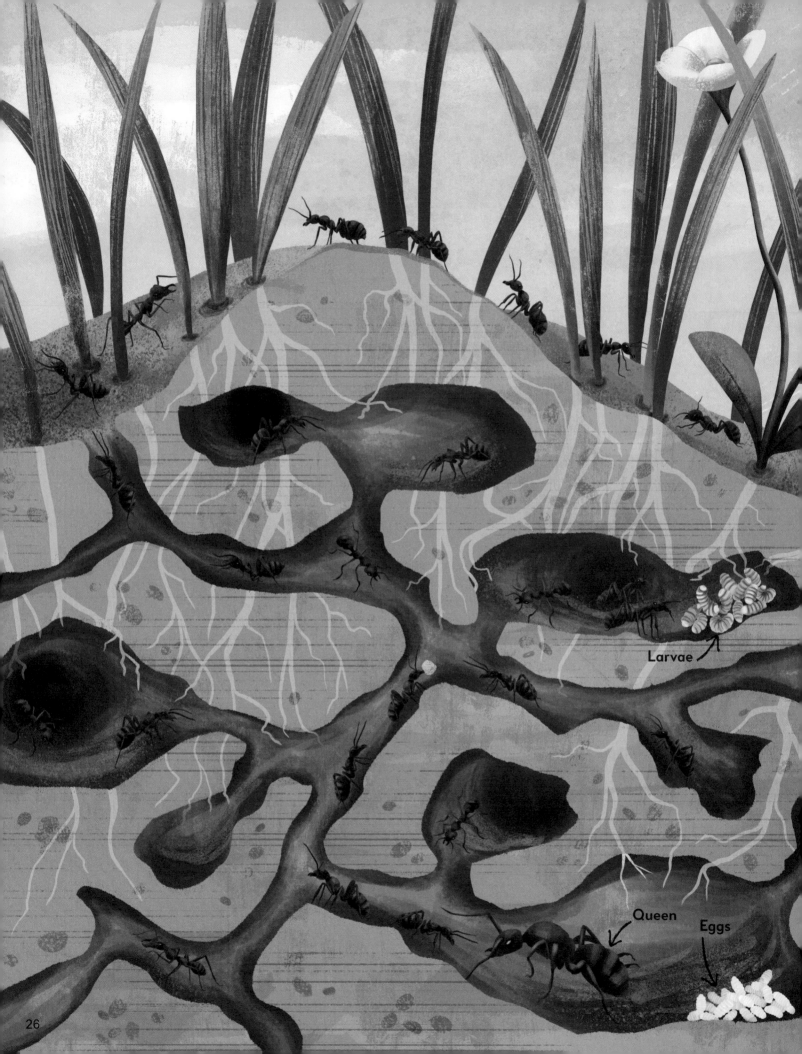

Larvae

Queen

Eggs

Ants

We are an army.

I am the queen ant and the largest ant, but I don't boss the other ants around. My job is to stay in the nest and lay eggs. The worker ants form a female army, and they decide what tasks to perform based on need. Young females care for me and our young—the eggs and larvae. Other workers dig tunnels, explore, and gather foods (we eat anything!), and soldier ants defend the nest against enemies. As the nest grows, worker ants will make new queens by feeding larvae high protein food made from chopped up food, unfertilized eggs, and their own saliva.

Soldier

Workers

"We love sugary food, and we'll leave a scent trail to tell the colony where to find it."

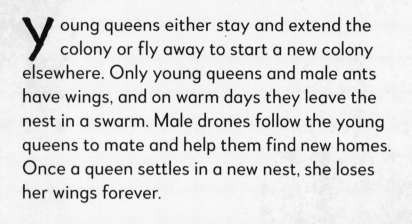

Young queens either stay and extend the colony or fly away to start a new colony elsewhere. Only young queens and male ants have wings, and on warm days they leave the nest in a swarm. Male drones follow the young queens to mate and help them find new homes. Once a queen settles in a new nest, she loses her wings forever.

We recognize one another by our individual scent, which we smell through our antennae and communicate by releasing chemicals called pheromones. Our smelly messages might say: "**Food this way**," or "**Rain. Take shelter,**" or "**Attack.**" If a predator or rival colony tries to invade the nest, an army of worker ants will mob, sting, spray, and bite the intruders.

Antennae

FACT FILE
Name of group: Colony
Size of group: 10-1,000,000
Fact: Ants are serious heavy lifters. They can carry 50 times their own body weight and they work together to move big objects.

Ants can also communicate using touch, and feel vibrations through their feet.

Drones only live for a few weeks.

Young queen

Emperor penguins

We are a colony of pairs.

Across the ice I waddle, one in a long line of penguins returning to the winter breeding grounds. It's time to partner up! **Trumpet! Trill! Squawk!** We bond with our partners by mimicking each other's movements, a slow mirror dance that lasts for days and builds trust.

After my partner lays our egg, she carefully passes it to me. I rest the egg on my feet and tuck it into my brood pouch. For 65 days I wait and huddle with the other dads, protecting our egg from the cold, while my partner returns to the sea to hunt and fatten up.

Male penguin

Winters in Antarctica are bitterly cold, so the egg needs to be kept as warm as possible.

Egg

Female penguin

Juveniles

It takes a few months for chicks to shed their fluffy feathers and become waterproof.

Just as the egg hatches, my partner returns, and I carefully pass her our chick to feed. By now, I am very hungry, so it's my turn to return to the sea to catch fish, fatten up, and return with the food.

For a while we take turns looking after our chick, but soon she gets so hungry that we both need to go hunting. When we do, we leave her in a chick daycare. By this time, it's summer, the ice is melting, and the walk to the sea isn't far. Once our chick sheds her fluffy feathers and becomes a juvenile, she is ready to go for her first swim!

FACT FILE

Name of group: Colony
Size of group: 1,000-20,000
Fact: Every winter, penguins return to the same breeding ground, and often choose the same partner.

"We help each other hunt, and look out for dangerous leopard seals and orcas."

European bison

We are a democracy.

I live in a big group called a herd, and we feel safe in one another's company. Most of the time the herd is made up of cows, calves, and young bulls. Mature bulls wander alone or hang out in small groups nearby, and visit us in the mating season.

The herd works together to look out for predators, such as wolves. We **snort** in alarm and protect our calves by surrounding them and lowering our horns. This usually makes the wolves change their mind. After all, we are a lot bigger than they are!

Defensive bison

Hungry wolf

Herd leader

Bison are the largest living land mammal in Europe—6.5ft (2m) tall by 10ft (3m) long.

Any cow can take a turn leading the herd. If I think the herd should move toward the river, I'll stop grazing and wander in that direction and see if others follow me. If most of the herd does, then they have decided I should lead them. But if most of the herd ignores me, then I didn't get the majority vote—at least not that time!

I can always try again another day. Sometimes the herd splits for a while if two cows want to go in opposite directions and have enough followers. We can always find each other again by following the herd's scent and **bellowing** to each other..

Other herd leader

"We love taking sand baths to clean our coats, and welcome oxpecker birds who peck biting insects from our skin."

FACT FILE

Name of group: Herd
Size of group: 10-30
Fact: European bison almost became extinct, but rewilding projects have since increased the population to around 7,000.

Crows

We flock together.

The first winter after I hatched, I flew in a great flock and explored the land. The older crows taught me where to peck for food, how we defend ourselves from hawks, and which trees to roost in. During the long winter nights, we huddled together for safety and warmth, and shared our knowledge. A roost has a pecking order. The older birds take the safest, coziest spots near the top of the tree, and the younger birds perch on the lower branches, where we have to put up with being pooped on!

"A crow never forgets a face."

"Cheep cheep!"

When spring came, I returned to the nesting tree to help my mother and father raise their chicks. My sister arrived too, and we raced each other to collect sticks and leaves for the nest. After two weeks of building the nest, my mother was ready to lay her eggs. She sat on the eggs to keep them warm, and we took turns guarding her and bringing food to the nest.

CRACK. One day, the first egg hatched, and I watched my little brother break free of his shell. Then four more hungry chicks hatched. Each day, we all flew back and forth with beaks full of seeds, worms, and beetles. The hatchlings grew quickly. Their fluffy feathers soon disappeared and were replaced by blackish-brown flight feathers. At just 30 days old they stood at the edge of the nest, ready to fly. And after a little practice, they joined us in the great flock in the sky.

"Caw caw."

FACT FILE

Name of group: Murder
Size of group: 100–100,000
Fact: When a crow dies, other crows gather around the dead bird to learn who or what killed it. If it was a predator, such as a cat, they band together in a mob, dive bomb, peck, and scold the cat until it runs away.

Honeybees

We are a hive mind.

I start life as a tiny egg laid by the queen in a hexagonal cell at the center of the nest. I hatch into a larva and my older sisters feed me royal jelly which makes me fat and sleepy. I spin a cocoon and over 12 days transform into a young female worker bee.

If the queen is nearing the end of her life. Worker bees create new queens by feeding a few larvae extra royal jelly. The first queen that hatches, stings her competitors and takes over the rule of the colony. The queen never leaves the nest unless the colony is threatened, then she will swarm with some of the worker bees and find a new home.

Every worker bee in the nest has a job to do and switches jobs as needed to maintain a healthy colony. As a house bee, I clean the cells ready for new eggs to be laid. I learn to make royal jelly for the larvae, and I mix pollen and nectar together to make food.

Our nest is getting crowded, so I become a builder bee. I create more cells to house the larvae and to store pollen, nectar and honey. Next, I join the honey-making team to turn the nectar into the honey that the colony will eat.

Worker bee

Builder
bee

Queen bee

Honey-making bee

"Buzzzz."

Stinger

"I make up to 12 collecting trips a day, and can visit 100 flowers each time."

As a guard bee, I take my first flight. I circle the nest and look out for invaders who want to steal our honey. I'll sting them if I have to, even though I'll die if I do. Lastly and most importantly, I become a collector bee. I can remember my way around the garden, and use the sun to guide me. I tuck pollen into the sacs on my legs and suck up nectar with my proboscis (straw-like tongue) and store it in a sac in my mouth. When I find a patch of flowers bursting with pollen, I fly back to the nest and do a special **waggle dance** to tell my sisters which direction to go to find it.

Collector bee

FACT FILE

Name of group: Colony
Size of group: 100-80,000
Fact: Male bees are called drones and they are cared for by female bees. As soon as they are ready to fly, they leave the hive to search for young queens and they do not live long after mating. A healthy queen can lay up to 2,000 eggs a day.

Seahorses

We are determined dads.

Seahorses are the only species where the male carries and gives birth to the babies.

Brood pouch

"We stay together for life."

Tail looping

Every morning we pair bond. We rise to the surface, spinning and changing color in a quivering dance to impress each other. My mate puts her eggs in my brood pouch, and I fertilize them and keep them safe. While we wait for the eggs to hatch, we spend our days hunting for food.

We loop our tails together to swim from one leaf to the next and then wrap our tails around a plant to stop from drifting away. To catch tiny fish and plankton, we change color and camouflage ourselves to look like part of the coral. We can suck up food from 1in (3cm) away with our long snouts.

Camouflage

When the eggs in my pouch have hatched, I push out all of the baby seahorses. They are independent from the moment they are born, and drift in the currents until they can hook their tails around a rock or plant to hide. Within days of my pouch being empty, my partner fills it again with her next batch of eggs. Baby seahorses are called fry. They are tiny and vulnerable in the big ocean. Not many make it to adulthood, so it's important for dads to keep having lots of babies.

Fry

"We can glide forward, backward, up, and down."

FACT FILE

Name of group: Herd
Size of group: 1,000–4,000
Fact: 5–1,000 fry are born at the same time, but less than 1 out of 100 will make it to adulthood.

Meerkats

We live by mob rule!

As the sun rises and warms the desert, I scamper out of my burrow and listen carefully. I sniff the air to check if an eagle, snake, or jackal is lying in wait. Then I take up position on top of a mound of earth, where I have a good view of both the desert and the sky. I am the first sentry of the day. While the mob forages and hunts for food, I watch out for predators. I constantly **hum** and **peep** to the mob to reassure them that everything is okay.

The mob scatters to sniff out beetles, caterpillars, fruit, and birds' eggs. My mate is the dominant female. She catches a scorpion, bites off its tail, and takes it back to the pups so they can practice eating food that pinches and stings. When we are above ground our pups are cared for by babysitters who will defend them with their lives.

"We spend a lot of time grooming and playing with one another to reinforce family bonds and loyalty."

Pups

50

Sentry

The sentry keeps watch to protect the group from danger.

Dominant female

Only the dominant female has pups and chooses her mate.

Eagle

Burrow

Venomous cobra

"Mobs are made up of lots of different families and groups."

An eagle passes overhead, and I call a warning. Meerkats have 10 different calls which we use to reassure and warn the mob. There is a different call for each type of predator, so the mob understands what the danger is.

The mob disappears into specially dug boltholes. The eagle isn't fast enough to catch us, and he soon moves on. After an hour, my mate takes my place on the mound, and it's my turn to hunt. A cobra slithers out of the shadows and I **squeak** in alarm. The mob runs to help, and together we bite and confuse the snake. The snake would kill a lone meerkat, or worse, slither into a burrow and eat our pups, but because we work together it becomes our dinner instead.

FACT FILE

Name of group: Mob
Size of group: 4-40
Fact: Sentries don't just look out for predators, they also look out for rival meerkat mobs who want to take their foraging territory and kill their pups.

Mexican free-tailed bats

We are a community cave roost.

We hunt at dusk—a dark column of fluttering wings soar into the sky! I break away, swooping and zigzagging after moths and flying beetles, **pip-pipping** high frequency sounds that bounce off the bugs like an echo. These echoes tell me where the bugs are and what they are doing. I also use my echolocation to find my way and to avoid crashing into other bats.

Moth

Sharp talons help bats
lock onto the rock.

Pups huddled
together for
warmth

FACT FILE

Name of group: Colony
(or cloud if in flight).

Size of group: 100-20 million

Fact: Mexican free-tailed bats are
some of the fastest fliers in the animal
kingdom, capable of traveling at up
to 60mph (95kph) and as high as
10,000 ft (3,000m).

During spring, we fly north from Mexico to Texas, where there are lots of tasty bugs to hunt. Once there, our colony separates into bachelor roosts for males and maternity roosts for pregnant females. The moms help each other raise the pups. When my pup is born, I catch him in my wings to stop him falling to the ground. We **pip** and **squeak** until we recognize each other's call and scent. Instinctively, my pup knows how to grip with his talons.

When I go hunting, I leave my pup high in the cave with the other pups where he is safe. When I return, I follow the sound of his call. He drinks my milk and eats the bugs I have brought. He grows quickly, and is soon flapping around the cave, testing his wings and echolocation. When the pups are ready to leave, we emerge in a cloud of thousands so that we confuse any snakes, raccoons, or owls that wait to snatch young bats at the mouth of the cave.

"We like to return to the same roost every year to have our pups."

Nile crocodiles

We are neighborly.

New hatchlings are kept safe in their mom's mouth.

Hatchlings

"Ump Ump Ump."

U mp. Ump. Ump. It's time to hatch. Tap. Tap. Tap. My egg tooth breaks the shell. **CRACK!** I roll into the sandy nest and greet my sisters and brothers. Our mother gathers us up into her mouth and takes us to the river for our first swim. Our father is the dominant male and patrols the river, guarding all his nests and hatchlings from rivals. We hide among the water plants calling to one another—it's safer together.

When our mother spots danger, she **hisses** and lunges at the threat, and calls us to swim back into her mouth for protection.

I'm a natural predator, and from the moment I'm born I instinctively know how to hunt. I snap at any creature that passes by, such as a dragonfly, a fish, or a lizard.

Dragonfly

Dominant male

Lizard

Sunbathing

"Stay away from the bank! I can hold my breath, move stealthily, and explode out of the water."

Lurking crocs can leap 10ft (3m) out of the water to grab prey.

As I grow, I learn patience. I hide just below the surface of the water and wait for prey to come close—then I lunge! My jaws wrap around my dinner and I drag the animal beneath the water, twisting and rolling until it's still.

When we are big enough, my mother pushes us away. There isn't enough food, and we must find our own stretch of river.

I am careful around the older crocodiles, who are the bosses of the river. They dominate the best spots with their size and enormous jaws.

Sometimes young crocs team up and we help each other to herd fish into our mouths and hold down big prey so the others can feed. We're good at taking turns, and afterward we love to sunbathe together on the bank.

Crocodiles may spend a lot of time sitting still, but they can run very quickly when they choose to!

FACT FILE

Name of group: Bask (or float if in water).

Size of group: Unknown

Fact: The Nile crocodile can live for up to 100 years. They eat anything they can get their jaws around, but they don't need to eat every day. In fact, they only need a big meal every two weeks.

Orangutans

We are super single moms.

My baby and I move as a pair. His grip is strong as he clings to my back, and we swing slowly from branch to branch searching for fruit.

At the end of each day—before it gets too dark—I build a tree nest high in the canopy for us to sleep on where we are safe from prowling leopards. My baby helps, learning which branches are strong and which will snap. If it rains, it's hard to sleep, so we find big leaves to use as umbrellas.

When we find a durian or mango tree, we stop to eat and rest. I show my baby how to crack open the tough skins and teach him which fruits are good to eat. He is slowly learning where to find food at different times of the year. One day, he will live alone, and I must teach him everything he needs in order to know to survive.

When lots of fruit ripens in one place, orangutans gather together. We meet other mothers and babies, and sometimes groups of young adults who help each other until they are ready to wander the forest alone. We greet each other with **purrs** and share food. Only the dominant male fights with other males to keep his territory.

"All the females think the dominant male's saggy throat sacks and cheek flanges are very impressive!"

Dominant male

FACT FILE

Name of group: Congress or buffoonery

Size of group: Orangutans rarely group together in large numbers for long. They prefer to live alone or in small groups of two or three.

Fact: Orangutans are the largest arboreal (tree-dwelling) animals on Earth. An orangutan mom cares for her baby for seven to ten years, which is the longest childhood dependence on a mother in the animal kingdom.

Meet the loners

These solitary animals prefer to eat, sleep, and hunt alone. Male and females only get together when it's time to mate.

Male tiger

TIGER

I live in a large territory that overlaps with the territory of female tigers. When the females have my cubs, I protect them from a distance. I roam my territory and attack any tiger who enters. I must win, or competitors will take over the right to mate with the females and kill my cubs.

A tiger's territory must have water to drink, dense vegetation for hiding in, and prey to catch.

"We will defend our territory to the death."

PLATYPUS

I forage at night and spend much of the day snoozing in my riverside burrow. I don't pay any attention to the female or young platypuses in the river unless it's mating season. If a rival male swims by and tries to take over my territory, I fight him and scratch him with the venomous spurs on the back of my legs until he gives up.

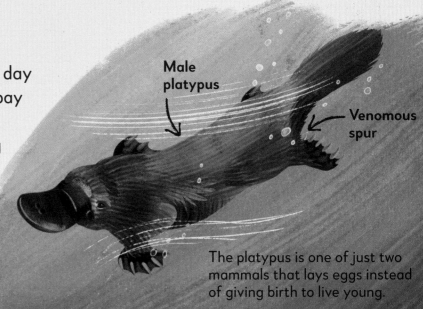

Male platypus

Venomous spur

The platypus is one of just two mammals that lays eggs instead of giving birth to live young.

Female koala

Joey

KOALA

When my joey was born, she stayed in my pouch and drank my milk until she was strong enough to cling to my back as we moved from tree to tree. When she was old enough to take care of herself, she found a territory near mine. Male koalas **bellow** to tell us they want to mate and where they are. They rub their tummies on trees and leave a scent to mark their territory.

"We take care of our babies until they are old enough to leave."

MOLE

I dig lots of underground tunnels in search of juicy worms. Other moles are not welcome in my territory, but males sometimes visit to mate. When I am expecting pups, I dig out a new room called a fortress, and line it with leaves. I take care of my pups for five weeks and then make them leave. They head above ground in search of an unoccupied yard or field, and must hide from predators such as owls, rats, weasels, and foxes until they can dig new underground homes.

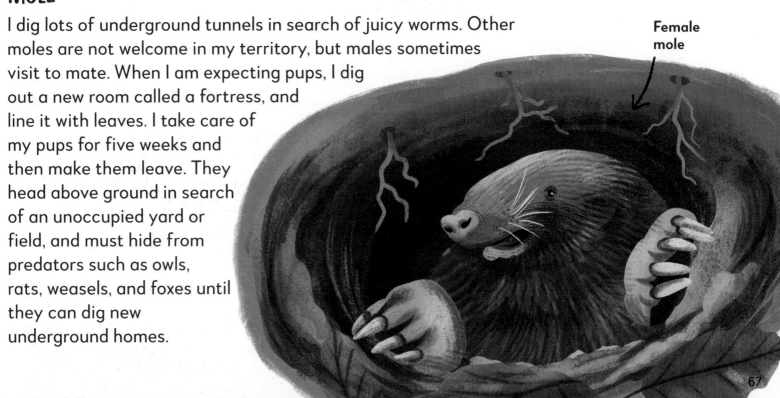

Female mole

Female large
blue butterfly

LARGE BLUE BUTTERFLY

I lay my egg on a plant near a red ant's nest. When my caterpillar hatches, he looks and smells like an ant larva, and creates a sugary food that attracts worker ants. The ants think he is one of their own and take him back to their nest. They house him with their larvae, which my caterpillar then eats. When he is fat enough, he spins a cocoon and pupates. The cocoon is safe from predators in the ant nest while my larva metamorphoses into a butterfly.

"We trick other animals into raising our young."

CUCKOO

I lay my eggs in the nests of other birds when they are away finding food. I'll even push out one of their eggs to make room for mine. My chick hatches first and instinctively nudges out any remaining eggs or hatchlings. As she is the only chick, the host parents don't realize, and she grows much bigger and stays longer in the nest than their chicks would. By the time the host parents realize they have a cuckoo in the nest, it's too late—my chick has grown her adult feathers and is ready to fly.

Baby
cuckoo

Cuckoo eggs mimic the shape
and color of other birds' eggs.

Only a very small number of baby sea turtles will survive until adulthood.

Turtle hatchling

SEA TURTLE

Each summer, I return to the same beach where I hatched to lay my own eggs. I dig a hole and cover my eggs with sand, so they are hidden from birds and lizards. Then I head back to the ocean and don't return. When the eggs hatch, the baby turtles crawl out of the sand and race to the sea as fast as they can.

"Our babies are on their own from the moment they are born."

GREAT WHITE SHARK

When my pups are ready to be born, I swim to a place I know is sheltered and has lots of fish to eat. My pups are independent sharks as soon as they are born, and they instinctively know how to hunt. A hormone in my body suppresses my need to hunt so I'm not tempted to eat my own pups— but I swim away quickly just in case!

Baby great white shark

Baby great white sharks can be up to 5ft (1.5m) long at birth.

A mom and dad family

A family with two dads

What about humans?

Our communities can be large, small, or any size in between!

A family with two moms

A single mom family

A single dad family

A stepfamily

Human families, just like animal families, come in all types and sizes. Lots of people live with their family, but many others live alone, as a couple, or with friends. And in human groups, people of any gender can be leaders and do any job.

"We are the most flexible species on the planet, and family is very important to us."

A foster or adopted family

An extended family

Conclusion

I hope you enjoyed meeting the animal families in this book and discovering that there are all kinds of families.

Imagine if you could spend a day as a member of an animal family. Which animal would you choose, and what would your role in the family be?

Perhaps you'd be a **lioness** responsible for finding food, or the **head chimpanzee** in charge of the troop.

What about the **young dolphin** ready to join a friendship pod and explore, or the **meerkat sentry** protecting the community from danger?

Just like animal families, the people in a human family have different roles and responsibilities, too. Sometimes these are shared. Think about your own family...

Who's who?

- Who's the bossiest?

- Who makes the important decisions?

- Who usually makes dinner?

- Who's the most playful?

- Who's the most caring?

Ask each member of your family the same questions. Do they agree? Would anyone like to change their role?

> I want to be in charge!

Meet an **ethologist**: a scientist who studies the behavior of animals. They choose a species that interests them, and watch them living their lives in the wild. They study both family groups and individuals, and collect lots of data—sometimes over many years. It's this information that helps us to understand why animals do what they do every day.

Glossary

Antennae

Long, thin organs on the heads of insects and crustaceans that are used to feel.

Bachelor

A young animal who has left its parent group and not yet formed or found a new one.

Body language

The gestures and movements an animal uses to communicate.

Bolthole

A hole in an animal's home used for escape.

Brood pouch

A pouch or hollow area in animals such as frogs and fish, where their eggs develop and hatch.

Canopy

The second from top layer of a rainforest, where many animals live among the trees.

Cheek flanges

Large cheek pads found on dominant male orangutans that make them more attractive to females.

Colony

A group of animal species that lives together.

Democracy

Groups that make collective decisions or offer each individual the opportunity to express themselves in the community.

Dominant

Being commanding over others, or the leader in a group.

Durian

A large, oval-shaped, prickly fruit from Southeast Asia.

Echolocation

A process some animals use to locate objects with sound rather than sight.

Egg tooth

A temporary tooth that helps a chick break through its eggshell and hatch.

Hatchling

A young bird or animal that has recently hatched from its egg.

Hive mind

The collective activity of a colony of social insects, such as bees or ants, that functions like a single mind.

Hormone

A chemical substance that sends messages to parts of the body, telling it what to do.

Joey

A young koala.

Juveniles

Young animals that are not yet fully grown.

Larvae

Insects or animals, such as frogs, that have left the egg, but have not yet developed into adults.

Low-frequency

Low, deep noises that are below the range that human ears can usually detect.

Maternity

Providing care during and immediately before and after childbirth.

Matriarchal

A society ruled by females. Likewise, patriarchal societies are ruled by males.

Metamorphoses

When animals undergo extreme and fast physical changes after birth (such as a caterpillar turning into a butterfly).

Pair bond

A strong bond that develops between a mating pair. They will often reproduce together and their bond may be for life.

Pupate

To develop into a pupa, which is the stage between larva and adult, when the insect is contained by a hard covering, such as a cocoon.

Rewilding

Protecting an environment and returning it to its natural state, for example, by bringing back wild animals that used to live there.

Sacs

Pouches in animals or plants, which often contain a fluid.

Savanna

The name given to open grasslands in tropical and subtropical countries.

Stealthily

Doing things secretly and quietly.

Index

About the author

Kate Peridot is an author of both fiction and nonfiction children's books that inspire and enthrall young readers using immersive storytelling techniques. She writes books about animals, people, and STEM that encourage a can-do spirit, a quest for knowledge, and a sense of adventure.

Kate's research skills were honed by a love of books, studying for an international business degree, working as a marketer for food companies, and as a freelance writer. Kate started writing professionally 10 years ago with short fiction and articles for magazines. In 2014, her children's story, *The Elephant Carnival*, won a Walker Books Animal Stories competition for 4-7 year olds. She won The First Chapter of a Novel competition at the Winchester Literary Festival for a YA concept. She has completed writing courses at The London School of Journalism and Curtis Brown Creative, and is a member of SCBW and SOA.

Her debut nonfiction book, *Caring Conservationists Who Are Changing Our Planet* was published in spring 2023 and a further eight nonfiction titles are in production to be launched between 2022-2025.
Find out more at www.kateperidot.com

The author would like to thank

Becky Bagnell for calling this early book concept "genius." James Mitchem and all the team at DK for giving *My Animal Family* the opportunity to fly into the world and hopefully around it, too! Nic Jones for her super-colorful, boisterous, and busy illustrations of family life—the animal families really are every type and size. To my own wolf pack, Peter, Jessica, and Jack, who I always want to come home to and snuggle up with in our den at the end of a story-hunting day.

About the illustrator

Nic Jones is inspired by the intricacy and beauty of the natural world, and applies this to her illustration and design.

Her illustrations are influenced by a passion for traditional drawing techniques, and they combine rich, vivid colors with explorative, textured brushstrokes. Nic creates her bold illustrative work in Photoshop, and she has masterfully adapted her digital painting style to convey traditional illustration techniques, while maintaining the advantages of working digitally.

About the consultant

Dr. Nick Crumpton is a writer and zoologist based in London. He received his PhD in zoology from the University of Cambridge, has appeared as an expert on radio and television programs, and has worked for the BBC and the Natural History Museum London. He acts as a biological consultant for numerous publishing houses and lectures at University College London. He lives in London.
Find out more at www.nickcrumpton.com

The publisher would like to thank

Becky Bagnell for bringing us such a wonderful proposal, and her continued support. Jake Da'Costa for his tireless design help and organization—he's the best around. Alex Hadlow at The Artworks Illustration Agency. Lynne Murray for picture library assistance. Marie Lorimer for indexing.

DK | Penguin Random House

Author Kate Peridot
Illustrator Nic Jones
Consultant Dr. Nick Crumpton

Acquisitions Editor James Mitchem
Senior Designer Elle Ward
US Senior Editor Shannon Beatty
Project Art Editor Jacob Da'Costa and Intrepid Books LTD
Editor Becca Arlington
Production Editor Dragana Puvavic
Production Controller Leanne Burke
Jacket and Sales Material Coordinator Magda Pszuk
Jacket Designer Elle Ward
Deputy Art Director Mabel Chan
Publishing Director Sarah Larter

First American Edition, 2023
Published in the United States by DK Publishing
1745 Broadway, 20th Floor, New York, New York 10019

Copyright © 2023 Dorling Kindersley Limited
DK, a Division of Penguin Random House LLC
23 24 25 26 27 10 9 8 7 6 5 4 3 2 1
001–333322–May/2023

DK books are available at special discounts when purchased in bulk for
sales promotions, premiums, fund-raising, or educational use. For details, contact:
DK Publishing Special Markets, 1745 Broadway, 20th Floor, New York, New York 10019

Printed and bound in China

For the curious
www.dk.com

MIX
Paper | Supporting
responsible forestry
FSC™ C018179

This book was made with Forest
Stewardship Council™ certified
paper – one small step in DK's
commitment to a sustainable future.
For more information go to
www.dk.com/our-green-pledge